SEC RET STAYS

SUMMER
reading
LIST 2024

CELEBRATING
TWENTY-FIVE YEARS

J.P.Morgan

MELINDA STEVENS

in collaboration with
ISSY VON SIMSON and TABITHA JOYCE

SECRET STAYS

Pioneering Hosts of the New Chic

ASSOULINE

Table of Contents

6   Introduction

8   Lopud 1483   Francesca Thyssen-Bornemisza

24   Casa na Terra   Manuel Aires Mateus

36   Passalacqua   The De Santis family

52   Bethlen Estates   The Bethlen family

64   Aristide Hotel   The Aristide family

74   Villa Mabrouka   Jasper Conran

90   Boath House   Jonny Gent and Russell Potter

108   Cristine Bedfor   Cristina Lozano

118   Le Mas de Chabran   Alain and Liliana Meylan

128   Castle Elvira   Harvey B-Brown and Steven Riseley

140   Braganza House   Chlöe Elkerton

156   Taylor River Lodge   Chad and Blake Pike

170   *Maana Homes*   Hana Tsukamoto and Irene Chang

182   *Tizkmoudine*   Villagers of Tizkmoudine with the support of Thierry Teyssier

196   *Villa Cetinale*   The Earl and Countess of Durham

210   *Villa Palladio*   Barbara Miolini

220   *The Hall at Bolton Abbey*   The Duke and Duchess of Devonshire

234   *The Manor House, Babylonstoren*   Karen Roos and Koos Bekker

246   *Mesón Hidalgo*   Laura Kirar

258   *Villa Magnan*   Anne and Jérôme Israël

274   *Langdon Court*   Donna Ida Thornton and Robert Walton

286   *Castello di Reschio*   The Bolza family

300   *Properties*
302   *Acknowledgments & Credits*

Introduction

Earlier this year, I went to stay as part of a big house party with the owners of the Hall at Bolton Abbey in Yorkshire. On Saturday morning, I wandered its quiet corridors, a mouse on the march. Floors creaked, pigeons cooed like bubbling soup outside the window, quiet murmurings of pots on the boil coiled up from the kitchen. In the breakfast room, I poured coffee into a cup. I folded the back of a newspaper, snap. I looked at the huge oil paintings of pale-faced ancestors sitting moonishly alongside their eager hounds and imagined the hushed squeak of their barks and their tails' soft swish along the flagstones.

But mostly, it was silent. A special kind of silence that goes back in time and forward in time in a corridor of forever. The kind of silence that changes the position of things, that makes you realize it's the house that's living and you're no more than a cell within its bloodstream for this pocket-small moment in time.

The Hall belongs to the Duke and Duchess of Devonshire. It was built in 1678. And now it's open for revelers of all descriptions. For anyone who wants to suck up picnics on the moors, knee-deep in treacle tart and red wine, who hankers for walks, for landing a fat trout on the lawn, for pottering around the abbey, for pressing backs against the mossy walls of the kitchen garden and gorging on soft, sweet greengages.

The Hall is not alone in this endeavor. These usually private spots, these hidden homes, these mysterious castles, these outlandish *castelli* and *riads* and monasteries and châteaus, previously entirely inaccessible, have now flung open their doors. Partly motivated out of financial viability, it's also been made possible because society walls are being dismantled by a younger generation who have a new attitude, who are not scared of sharing, and who understand the power for all in being open-armed.

How one-dimensional these places have made run-of-the-mill hotels look! How wide-eyed and functional! Here is history, storytelling, fortunes won and lost, layers to experience. Here is something unique and of this place, and of this place alone! At one point in the hotel boom that began gathering real pace in the '90s, it looked like all we wanted to do was fly and flop. To have breakfast on the terrace with those little pots of honey and strawberry jam. To gorge on pillow menus and chocolate rooms and brunch on a tray that floated in the infinity pool attached to our overwater villa.

But it turned out we also wanted something else, and in the noughties, someone else made that possible. People were, strangely if you think about it, renting out rooms to complete strangers, from a tiny flat in Copenhagen to a farmhouse in Bulgaria. And suddenly, it was happening everywhere. And suddenly, everyone was doing it. Airbnb changed what we gave value to, and it changed how we behaved. We loved being in people's houses now, tucked up into their lives; we loved the immediacy of the experience, the privacy, the control, the person in the personality of the place.

Perhaps more importantly at the center of this cultural shift, this morphing shape of how we travel, has been the mighty retro-realization that we believe again in true hospitality. We have a desire to provide which goes far beyond the transactional. To take strangers in, to shelter them from the storm, to exchange stories of different lands, to break bread, to offer rest.

It is feasibly one of the simplest and most profound of human undertakings. And it is what the game-changing owners in this book do: open their doors to what are now the world's most remarkable places to stay.

Melinda Stevens

Lopud 1483

Owned by Francesca Thyssen-Bornemisza

Lopud, Croatia

"All you need is lateral thinking, and patience," according to art collector Francesca Thyssen-Bornemisza. It's been thirty years since her first visit to the abandoned monastery on the island of Lopud, in southern Croatia. Padre Pio Mario, the head of the Franciscan order in Dubrovnik, took her out on the slowest put-put fisherman's boat. When they turned the final corner into the bay, she recalls, "I was just absolutely dumbfounded that anything could be really quite that extraordinary." This was the route Saint Francis had taken on his way to the Holy Land, and in his wake, the Franciscans became the main providers of education and protection for the community. So the monastery itself is more like a fortress. "I always say to people that visit, 'Look at these walls. Don't imagine that Lopud was always so quiet and peaceful. This was a place of bloodshed and great battles.'" The restoration, too, was a great battle. The monastery had been abandoned for a hundred years and was in a state of total ruin. A year or so later, after signing a very simple lease agreement, Francesca was in Croatia with architect Frank Gehry. She managed to convince a police boat to take them over to Lopud. When he looked at the building, Gehry said, "Francesca, take your time with this. You need to really get to know it." Three decades later, after Francesca's numerous head-on collisions with the Institute for the Protection of Cultural Monuments, endless permissions applications and re-applications, and a huge scavenger hunt across the country to rescue original roof tiles and wooden beams, the spirit of the monastery is not only intact but revived. Outside the grounds, carob and olive and lemon trees are once again rustling—"British horticulturist Monty Don came and said this is the most amazingly well-kept garden he's ever seen." Inside, the historic spaces are bristling with new energy. Graffiti is celebrated. The monks' names, scribbled by the ancient latrines, are still visible, as are the Fascists' scrawls that say "Il Duce," the nickname for Mussolini, in the master suite. And Francesca has brought her own history too. "I always felt that I had been shortchanged by the way the family loot was distributed." Her father, Baron Hans Heinrich Thyssen-Bornemisza, alongside his fortune from steel and armaments, held one of the most important private collections of Western paintings from the thirteenth to the twentieth centuries. "I ended up with a massive haul of furniture from Villa Favorita [her father's Lugano residence], which no one else wanted and I kept in storage. So it's been a great, fabulous joy to bring those things into the monastery. And they make sense here. My father entertained kings and queens at the sixteenth-century dining table. People say, do you use it? Yes, of course we use it. It's solid. How many people do you think have danced on this table over the years?"

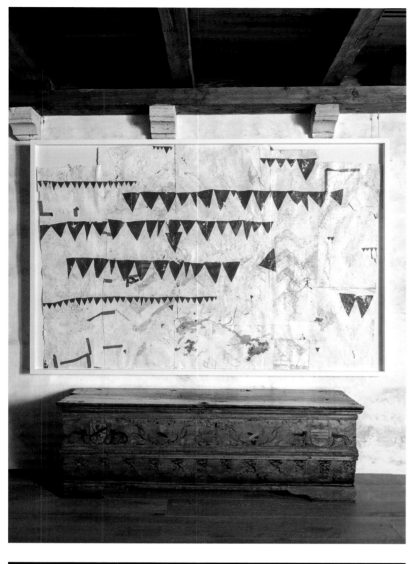

66 My father entertained kings and queens at the sixteenth-century dining table. People say, do you use it? Yes, it's solid. How many people do you think have danced on it over the years? **99**

Alentejo, Portugal

Casa na Terra

Owned by Manuel Aires Mateus

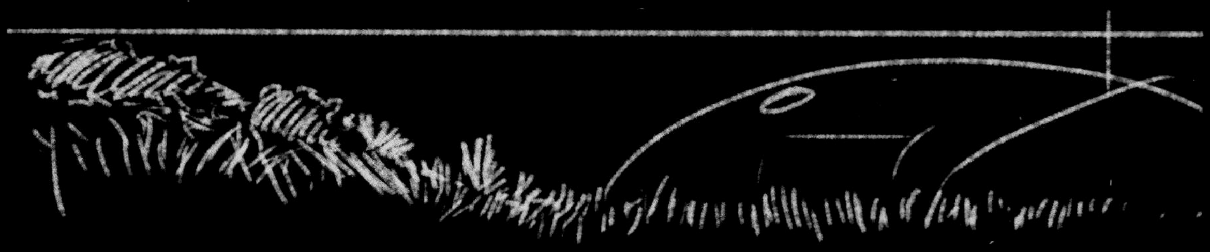

If you are more than a couple hundred meters away, you won't even see this subterranean house that melts into the remote Alentejo landscape, absolutely integrated with the color of the ground. But despite its lack of immediate physical presence, the lakeside bunker close to the border with Spain was more than a decade in the making. When the original owner went bankrupt, the architect working on the project, Manuel Aires Mateus, decided to buy the land and finish the job himself. The financial crisis then caused another roadblock and put the work on hold for four more years. At this point, the building was a concrete shell, and local rumors started to spread—the mysterious structure imagined as a bird-watching center or an observatory. "When we were finally able to pick the project up again, it was even more exciting because we were working with a sort of ruin," explains Manuel. The house is designed around the outside spaces—most noticeably the cobbled terrace facing the lake. "It's not a normal patio making the connection between the ground and the sky. Here we are making a connection with the water." It has a cantilevered ceiling with a perfect circle through which guests can stare at swallows swooping. And the area's Dark Sky status means that stars are bright enough to light the courtyard at night. "In the morning, because the house faces the sunrise, the first light comes through the water and the whole place turns gold." Inside, three bedrooms are minimalist with silky concrete floors, white tiles, and natural wood. And though Manuel has designed several next-level Portuguese rentals, this is by far his most personal. When his work was done and it was time to sell, which had always been the plan, his wife persuaded him not to. "It has a feeling of complete protection due to the heaviness of the ground above." And the longer it has had to settle into its surroundings, the more protected it feels.

❝ In the morning, because the house faces the sunrise, the first light comes through the water and the whole place turns gold. **❞**

Passalacqua

Owned by the De Santis family

Lake Como, Italy

Built in 1787, Passalacqua has seen some guests. Churchill and Napoleon both had sleepovers in the home of the Lucini Passalacqua family, who commissioned the palazzo. But the arts-obsessed owners were far more impressed by composer Vincenzo Bellini, who lived in their home and composed in the music salon for three years. Legend goes that his artistic muse, opera singer Giuditta Pasta, sang to Bellini across Lake Como, inspiring two of his most revered operas—*La Sonnambula* and *Norma*. More than two centuries later the De Santis family, of the locally beloved Grand Hotel Tremezzo, bought Passalacqua at an adrenaline-fueled private auction from an American banker, a sale which thrilled the locals. "There aren't many properties on the lake in the hands of Italians anymore," says Valentina De Santis, the third-generation owner and CEO of the palazzo, "and to have this one returned to a family so connected to the area is not something you see in the papers." The villa has a perspective that is completely different from that of any other hotel on Como: It's set much higher, above a terrace of formal olive, rose, and vegetable gardens, and cypress trees that line the way down to the water. There's even an underground tunnel connecting the ancient stables at the back of the villa to a private jetty on the lake that's completely hidden in the rock. When the De Santis clan took ownership of Passalacqua, they didn't work with a designer. "My parents are passionate antique lovers and would go off to auctions in Parma—leaving on a mission and coming back with trucks." Silks were handpicked from Venetian clothmaker Rubelli; mirrors were designed by a small family business, Barbini. "Very quickly it became like doing up our own home—we started making decisions with our heart and our belly." Original stuccowork and frescoes were all saved, but a fresh, more forward-thinking spirit is also on display: Valentina's good friend JJ Martin, of fashion brand La DoubleJ, inspired the poolside design with her rainbow-bright linens and dahlia-print umbrellas. It's as maximalist as Bellini's "Casta diva" aria, as fun as Ferragosto, all year round.

66 My parents are passionate antique lovers and would go off to auctions in Parma— leaving on a mission and coming back with trucks. We started making decisions with our heart and our belly. 99

" There aren't many properties on the lake in the hands of Italians anymore, and to have this one returned to a family so connected to the area is not something you see in the papers. "

Bethlen Estates

Owned by the Bethlen family

Transylvania, Romania

The village of Criş is on the way to nowhere, halfway along a valley in what's often described as the last great wilderness in Europe. The imposing medieval Bethlen Castle sits on a hill above the hamlet, and beyond it the land opens into vast meadows and thick forests. At night, the stars are piercingly bright. This part of Transylvania has been this way for centuries. For Nikolaus Bethlen, it's his ancestral home. His family built the Renaissance-style castle and the beginnings of the village around the middle of the fifteenth century. "My father, Count Miklós Bethlen, grew up and lived in Transylvania until the Second World War forced him to flee. The castle was taken away and nationalized in 1947. It fell into disrepair and was used for potato storage." Nikolaus grew up in Austria, but during his childhood he and his parents returned to Transylvania for holidays, even when the country was behind two iron curtains. He developed an unbreakable bond with the place. "I wanted to have a house here for my young family and for my children to know where their roots are," he explains. Many of the buildings in the village lay empty (having been abandoned by Saxons who moved back to Germany in the early 1990s). They were dormant, hibernating. "I wanted to save them from being renovated with plastic windows from China and bright red paint." Nikolaus then found himself playing "a little bit of real-life Monopoly. I was meant to be creating a family home for myself, but somehow I ended up with more houses than family members." What he did then, and is still doing, is slowly, methodically breathing life into these village buildings, big and small—a hay barn, a piggery, a granary, the former German school—and creating a little network of homes, for his family but also for guests. Nikolaus has chosen every single book that lines the cases, picked all of the LPs for the record players dotted around, chosen figurines and knickknacks to decorate the shelves. Part of it is a desire to redeem what was destroyed, to make sure that the Bethlen legacy lives on. And part of it is the irresistible nature of the project. "Some people collect cars. I collect ruins."

66 My father, Count Miklós Bethlen, grew up and lived in Transylvania until the Second World War forced him to flee. The castle was taken away in 1947. I wanted to have a house here for my young family and for my children to know where their roots are. 99

Aristide Hotel

Owned by the Aristide family

Syros, Greece

The ferry that chugs over from Athens to Ermoupoli docks just steps from the grand neoclassical town hall. It could be this, or the marble pavements, perhaps the miniature La Scala, or maybe the old Venetian-style mansions, but Syros always feels stately and unexpected. It has a sense of restrained calm but also a highbrow wink. Romanian-Yemeni-Greek economist Oana Aristide felt like she'd "found a place that had been accidentally overlooked." She used to spend every summer here with friends, and then one year, her sister Jasmin and mother, Simona, joined and fell under its spell too. The plan was to buy a small holiday apartment, but "things got a little out of hand," she says, laughing. "We had been doing viewings for months, and in a fit of exasperation our estate agent told us, 'There's nothing for sale here except that house. And that's not for you—it's seven times your budget.'" The 1920s palazzo was built as a family home for a Greek shipowner. By the 1980s, it had become the Cycladic Tax Office. It had a beautifully carved marble staircase and Doric columns, but "these good bones had been completely abandoned. It was empty. No pieces of furniture, no art, nothing was left behind except some filing cabinets." There was, of course, a commitment to keeping all the original details and architecture, the ceiling decorations, the height of the rooms, but Oana did a sidestep on the interiors. Rich greens and blues are punctuated with sunshine yellows. "It was the only skepticism from our neighbors, that we were so bold with colors, but I felt there was no need to keep everything white." Instead of feeling like a museum, it's a contemporary home, but also a contemporary gallery. Artists come and stay at the hotel for up to three weeks. Some are right at the start of their careers and not known at all. Others, like Spanish fine-arts painter Salustiano, cause a bit of a stir and require extra security for their work. Oana has created a joyful cultural crash pad. Guests have their portraits painted after courtyard breakfasts of Greek yogurt, thyme honey, and figs. And in the evenings, there are Cycladic wine tastings and farm-to-table dinners on the rooftop, while you watch the ships come in.

66 We had been doing viewings for months, and in a fit of exasperation our estate agent told us, 'There's nothing for sale here except that house. And that's not for you—it's seven times your budget.' 99

Villa Mabrouka
Owned by Jasper Conran

Tangier, Morocco ✗

"Everyone was very curious because, having been private, nobody's been able to go near the property for about thirty years." The place in question, Villa Mabrouka, has had a storied past as the former home of Yves Saint Laurent and Pierre Bergé. "And before that," reveals British designer Jasper Conran, the new master of the house, "it was owned by a Kuwaiti princess." It's no wonder it mustered intrigue and curiosity. Sitting above the Bay of Tangier with wide-screen views across the Strait of Gibraltar, its huge grounds a riot of palm trees and bougainvillea, the villa has a magnetic pull. "I didn't come to Tangier with the intention of buying a house," Jasper professes. "I was looking for a tent." In 2018, he got swayed off course by an antiques-dealer friend, who whisked him up to take a look. It wasn't really on the market, not publicly anyway, and was being looked after by the Fondation Jardin Majorelle after Bergé's death. Inside, almost everything had been sold, so Jasper "pretty much had to start again." But he hasn't strayed far from Yves and Pierre's vision. The house was expanded but remains a pared-down retreat, calm, exquisite, understated, with little art on the walls. "I couldn't imagine a painting in the house. I did try. But it just wouldn't play ball with me." The building talks loudly enough for itself, in several languages, with Moroccan architecture and a 1940s spirit. "Then I've put in seventeenth-century Andalusian tiles and Roman mosaics, some North African antiques, and some modern things. It's a mix-up, a Tangier mash-up, a Conran-Bergé-Saint Laurent fusion." The garden does most of the talking in terms of color and vibrancy, whether it's banana trees right outside bedroom windows or the smell of wisteria or the sea, always there in view. "It's a very dominant force within the house, and I wanted to be responsive to that." When in 1997, Yves Saint Laurent and Pierre Bergé enlisted Jacques Grange to decorate the house, their design brief was to create the home of "an eccentric 1950s Englishman who had come to live in Tangier." Jasper laughs. "Well, now it is. Isn't that brilliant?"

66 When in 1997, Yves Saint Laurent enlisted Jacques Grange to decorate the house, the design brief was to create the home of 'an eccentric 1950s Englishman who had come to live in Tangier. Well, now it is. Isn't that brilliant?' 99

Nairn,
Scotland

Boath House

Owned by Jonny Gent and Russell Potter

While staying with his friend Tilda Swinton outside of Nairn, artist Jonny Gent—more used to working in studios all round the world—fell in love with the northeast of Scotland. "The skies are just so big here." He quickly bought an old cabin on the river next to a castle and turned it into a working gallery. "It became my car salesman's trick. I would invite collectors up to come and stay with me, get them drunk, take them fishing, and forage for mushrooms. I'd always have a great sound system, and by the time I unveiled the painting they barely had a choice." This was the moment he realized the power of the connection between food, music, and art. His elegantly dilapidated London restaurant/gallery, Sessions Arts Club, followed, "but I always knew that the Highlands had to be the headquarters." Jonny swiftly snapped up a Georgian manor house just ten minutes from his Scottish cabin. The phones and TVs were ripped out as soon as he got the keys. He also sold every piece of furniture in the house to a local antiques dealer—"I needed to see it empty"—only to return to the guy three months later to buy bits of it back at a higher price. Jonny's aim wasn't to create a hotel, so while you can book a night's stay, he sees Boath House as a studio with a seasonal residency program. All that he asks is that the artists, chefs, and writers who visit leave something behind. "I never wanted to fill it with art from the off. I can't really stand decoration. But I do love the idea that over time the memories create themselves." Country musician Courtney Marie Andrews bestowed a painting, the Darkness wrote an album here, and fashion designer Hannah Cawley of Cawley Studio took all of the restaurant's food waste and turned it into dyes to use in her clothing line. The added bonus is that when there's someone in residence, there's a focal point. "It's a trigger for conversation, and guests feel like they're peering behind the curtain." There's also the best restaurant for miles, dishing up plates of pickled cucumbers from the walled vegetable patch, bowls of damsons from the orchard, and local game. Children charge around the garden, playing table tennis and jumping into the burn, one of the cleanest in the country, filled with salmon and trout. "I start all of my projects with a word. Sessions was about sanctuary, and Boath is all about healing—if you're not quite there creatively, and then you do something you wouldn't normally, like wild swimming or fishing, it can be a magical, inspiring thing."

66 I never wanted to fill it with art from the off. I can't really stand decoration. But I do love the idea that over time the memories create themselves. 99

Cristine Bedfor

Owned by Cristina Lozano

✕ Mahón, Menorca

"I really don't mind if someone comes down in their pajamas for breakfast," says Cristina Lozano. The idea of creating a hotel and making it like a private house was a long-running joke for the Bilbao-born former journalist at dinner parties: "I'll be the maître d', you can be the housekeeper," she'd say to friends. After years of spending the night at various B&Bs around the Cotswolds while her sons were at school in Oxford, she started to solidify the idea: to create that feeling of being part of the family, but with some extra service on top; not complicated, but a little spoiling. "Mahón felt just perfect for this because it has such British heritage"—the island was under British rule for the better part of the eighteenth century. Cristina found a tiny town-house hotel with seven rooms for sale, and a hostel next door, and another house on the street. After a little negotiation, she bought the three, and her great friend designer Lorenzo Castillo set about creating the dialed-up-to-eleven English-country-house interiors: tapestries on the walls, mahogany antiques, and flea-market finds that Cristina picked up on trips to the South of France. "He's a genius with the fabrics, the mix that he makes." The look is layered, textured, full of color—a flip side to the usual Balearic bohemian whites and wicker. "We thought that if you have a house in the middle of Mahón, in the historic part of the city, you have to pay your respects to its roots." And even though it's got that slightly buttoned-up smartness, everyone is relaxed enough to kick off their shoes and settle in. "We have regular guests who've been coming since we opened because they were building villas on the island. Now the work is done, the builders are finished, and yet they're still at the hotel. They come with their dogs and their children—it makes me laugh." The philosophy that it should feel like a second home is working, then. And the guests are her friends? "That's the spirit—friends! But they pay! And they keep on saying, 'Thank you for having me,' too."

❝ I really don't mind if someone comes down in their pajamas for breakfast. We have regular guests who come with their dogs and their children. And they keep on saying 'Thank you for having me,' too. **❞**

Le Mas de Chabran

Owned by Alain and Liliana Meylan

Provence, France

It was horses that first brought keen riders Alain and Liliana
Meylan to Les Baux-de-Provence, but it was this four-hundred-year-
old *mas,* right next door to their holiday villa, that persuaded
the couple to move here from Geneva for good. "We knocked down
a lot of walls," says interior designer Liliana of the vaulted
former olive-oil mill. The house had seen various renovations, some
not as sympathetic as others, and the bathrooms were covered in pink
mirroring. Alain is an architect. His studio produces highly modern,
minimal residential buildings in Switzerland with lots of glass and
cantilevering, so this was quite the pivot for him. "He works from
the inside out, which is very unusual." During the project, the
couple discovered an entire floor not visible from the outside. "It
was completely blocked off, and it turned out that a former owner
had kept birds in there." Their goal was to connect with the serenity
of the place: Unconventional dark colors help frame the views from
the windows—of the ancient olive groves and the foothills of the
Massif des Alpilles. The house rejects all the expected Provençal
design tropes. The walls are covered in a clay-sand plaster using
local pigments: The deep ocher comes from Roussillon, the Orange
City, and the browns were taken from the soil. "I wanted to avoid
the imitation of old but without erasing the past altogether,"
Liliana explains. There is a heft to the style of the house now,
an elevated seriousness, with statement works of art and a moody
palette. "I don't like it when people come inside a house and can
spot the designer immediately. I hate that copy and paste on various
projects. I really think the area has to create the conditions for
a project. Then, of course, comes the personality of the person
living in it." In the gardens, the feeling of the South of France
returns. The grounds are dotted with stone fountains and lily ponds
and a henhouse, where you'll find Liliana's mother as early as five
a.m. collecting eggs. Then she'll pick melons, strawberries, and
mint for breakfast. There are majestic century-old plane trees and
the sun shines year-round, "but you feel the presence of the house
everywhere—we feel tiny next to it."

"During the project, the couple discovered an entire floor not visible from the outside. 'It was completely blocked off, and it turned out that a former owner had kept birds in there.'"

Castle Elvira

Owned by Harvey B-Brown and Steven Riseley

Puglia, Italy

People used to come from all over the world to seek respite in this part of Puglia, right on the heel of Italy's boot. There's an ancient monastery across the road from the castle, which was a former tuberculosis sanatorium. And this folly was commissioned by a father whose young daughter, Elvira, suffered from the disease. "It was built out of complete love," says owner, artist, and filmmaker Harvey B-Brown, who once designed for fashion label Red or Dead and produced extravagant window displays for Harvey Nichols and Liberty of London. Sadly, Elvira died and her father couldn't bear to be near the castle, and so it was left abandoned for 120 years. "We almost had to machete our way down the drive," Harvey says of his first visit with husband Steven Riseley. "But when we saw the castle, it was like you could hear angels singing. Steven still says in some ways that's the most beautiful he's ever seen it." The windows were bricked up, but people had still managed to get in and the walls had graffiti all over. "Luckily, the ceilings are so high they couldn't reach them." There was no electricity and no water, and the restoration job was huge, but the pair managed to preserve all of the original ceiling frescoes and they studied flakes of paint on the walls to try and repaint with something comparable. The result is a bold design, a contrast to the whitewashed Puglian trulli that dominate the scene here. "I've worked as a set designer and in fashion, and I've just never felt the boundary between these things." Harvey's art hangs on the walls, and he runs drawing classes for the guests. The wild gardens took some serious work too: "The weeds grew within thirty seconds of turning your back on them." And when they started clearing the vegetation, they discovered whole structures buried beneath. Now there are bedrooms inside a once hidden tower and in an old *masseria* that looks like a mini-cathedral inside. "It just felt like everything in the castle was magic and everything we unlocked had a new secret and a sense of wonder." It's almost like being at the end of the world here, atop a hill on a peninsula between two seas, with eight winds crisscrossing from all directions.

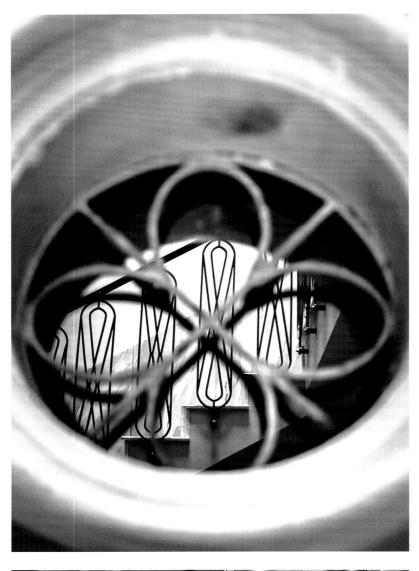

"The windows were bricked up, but people had still managed to get in and the walls had graffiti all over. 'Luckily, the ceilings are so high they couldn't reach them.'"

Talpe, Sri Lanka ✗

Braganza House
Owned by Chlöe Elkerton

There's always a bit of gentle grumbling about the huge round window in the main bedroom that looks out onto thick, pea-green jungle—there are no curtains! What about shutters? But Chlöe Elkerton steadfastly holds her ground. "I won't put anything there because I absolutely love waking up when the sun is rising. The trees start to rustle with monkeys. The chorus of the birds swells. Quite often a peacock will strut past. Once you've seen that, you never regret that it's only 5:30 a.m." Days at the house, up in the hills above the beach road, are punctuated by the soft jangle of Sri Lankan life. The sounds of the temple and the call to prayer drift on the breeze, the bread guy tootles past—his tuk-tuk playing tinkly tunes like an ice cream truck—and the nearby dog clinic provides the occasional howl and woof. In the air, there's the smoky musk of incense burning somewhere and the sweet tang of papayas fallen from the trees in the garden. And the house itself is just as prepossessing. The Sussex-born, Singapore-based interior designer's home speaks to the traditional local architectural vernacular of open-sided, thick-walled bungalows, cool even in the stifling heat. Wild blasts of color and pattern, pops of Beata Heuman and Penny Morrison, rub up against island antiques sourced by the brilliant Gamini in Thalpe. A pair of forest-green, twisted-barley four-poster beds, made by a team of skilled local artisans, have become a kind of viral hit, which Chlöe rolls her eyes at. Inspired by travels to the Caribbean, Greece, and Morocco, she has brought a bright-eyed energy to the place, though she insists the pace is as slow as you want it to be. "At breakfast it's hopper pancakes all around, and you can't move afterward, even if you want to." Christening the house Braganza felt inevitable: "My mum has a cottage in St. Mawes, Cornwall, which she bought shortly after my dad died. The beautiful Georgian house next door was called Braganza, and it had amazing views out to sea. I used to try to peek in through the massive old gates. I couldn't get the name out of my head." The House of Braganza just so happened to be the ruling dynasty for the last few decades of Portuguese Ceylon, in the early seventeenth century. Chlöe smiles. "It all felt aligned."

66 I won't put any curtains on the huge round window in the main bedroom because I absolutely love waking up when the sun is rising. The trees start to rustle with monkeys. The chorus of the birds swells. Quite often a peacock will strut past. Once you've seen that, you never regret that it's only 5:30 a.m. **99**

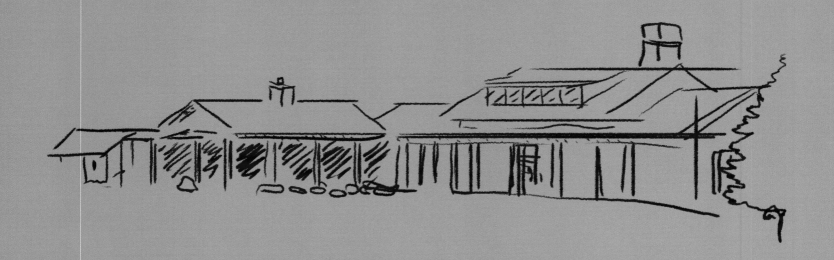

Taylor River Lodge

Owned by Chad and Blake Pike

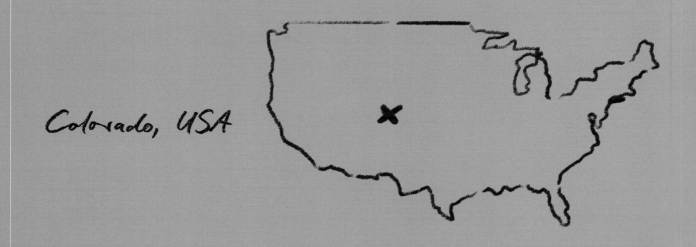

Colorado, USA

For years, Chad Pike was the head of a punchy global real estate business, but he was always a Huckleberry Finn inside, someone who gets "a bit scratchy" while sitting around in cities. His side hustle, a kind of hush-hush, unpredictable link of lodges in great landscapes, focused on getting busily immersed in nature, and it became the talk of the travel industry. Deplar Farm in Iceland and others in Harbour Island, Patagonia, and New Zealand are known for fun, cool, high-octane adventures for the plugged-in who want to go off-grid, clean of bed, dirty of hand, full of heart. And in Colorado, following on from his Wild West saloon in Crested Butte, which felt a little "urban," Chad went on the hunt for something more remote. "We drove out one day to Taylor Canyon. It's a tight canyon, with a freestone flowing river. And it's just so special. The main log cabin was an old general store for fishing and tackle, and it has this great vibe. The noise of the river is like a freight train, a roaring sound machine. And your blood pressure drops just like that." Being in charge "is a lot of work, though," Chad says, laughing. "What seems romantic and easy to do is not necessarily that straightforward." Chad's wife, Blake, decorated the lodge. The look is a highly elevated take on a dude ranch, with wood paneling, huge stone fireplaces, bearskin rugs, and a horseshoe-shaped bar. "She figures it out. It's the way we like to live. It's more of a camp, cozy with blankets and throws and low-key natural colors. It has a Rocky Mountain feel. But really, it's all about celebrating the outside." With no light pollution and a jet-black night, the sky is blanketed in stars. The people who stay here get gently pushed out of their comfort zone—part Scout camp, part frontier retreat. But wherever you go on the property, you can't escape the din of the water. "Big rivers have a feeling about them," says Chad, whose favorite spot is a pool above the bridge, where the trout seem to be particularly juicy. "There's a movement about them, the way the air flows. They're dangerous and they're wondrous."

66 We drove out one day to Taylor Canyon. It's a tight canyon, with a freestone flowing river. The noise of the river is like a freight train, a roaring sound machine. And your blood pressure drops just like that. 99

Kyoto, Japan

Maana Homes
Owned by Hana Tsukamoto and Irene Chang

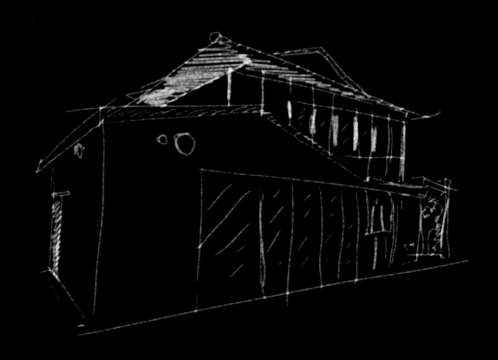

When Hana Tsukamoto moved from Japan to boarding school in California aged twelve, her first friend was Irene Chang. But it wasn't until more than twenty years later, having quit her job as an art director in New York to return home to Japan, that she thought about working with Irene, by then a designer based in L.A. Despite the sixteen-hour time difference, they hatched a plan to create something that filled the space between a hotel and an Airbnb. "There were no standards in Airbnb at the time, and we wanted to take that experience and make it better," says Hana. So they set about renovating a *machiya* town house in Kyoto. "I didn't really grow up here, so it was my first exposure to these beautiful traditional buildings." Part of their mission was to inspire the locals to appreciate the architecture. "The older a building is here, the less it's worth. Usually people only buy these places to knock them down and start again. It's crazy." There are now three homes in the collection, and although exposing the original wooden structures was a priority, the duo have pushed the boundaries on the design inside. "We literally got on our hands and knees to show the plasterers we wanted streaks and imperfections, which they found very hard to comprehend." And *washi* paper, usually for making lanterns, has been used on the walls, ceilings, and floors. "It's a lot more durable than people think, and it creates this really warm cocoon." At the same time as doing up the houses, Hana founded design brand POJ Studio to make available the new generation of Japanese craftsmanship she was discovering. Inside the riverside Maana Kamo, a handcrafted *shigaraki* bath is the centerpiece. "I don't think people realize you can design your own tub. It's so exciting to bring artisans in, and instead of churning out the same pieces, we work with them on something completely new." This ethos extends to the Maana experience too. The team sets up traditional Japanese breakfast deliveries of rice, miso, and fish and sends guests off to *kintsugi*-repair workshops or incense-making classes. The whole project is about ensuring the survival of pieces of heritage that feel like they could disappear. "I'm just happy if we inspire younger generations to look at our houses and actually want to live there."

" The older a building is here, the less it's worth. Usually people only buy these places to knock them down and start again.
It's crazy. **"**

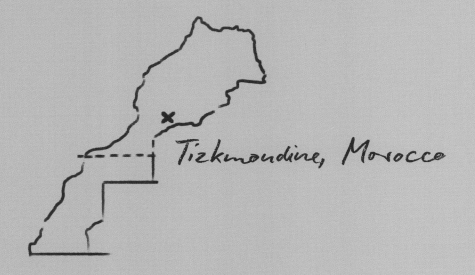

Tizkmoundine, Morocco

Tizkmoundine

Owned by the villagers of Tizkmoundine with
the support of Thierry Teyssier

Former stage director Thierry Teyssier made a name for himself when he restored a casbah in Morocco and turned it into the trailblazing Dar Ahlam, his first regenerative tourism project and a way to preserve a historical building at risk. Then came 700'000 Heures, the Paris-born creative's nomadic hotel, which has taken travelers to a traditional fishing village near Kyoto and glamping on sand dunes in Brazil, the destination changing every few months. "I realized during those wanderings that the most amazing moments—the happiest ones, the most natural ones—were with communities." And then he got a call from Global Heritage Fund, which had finished restoring a granary inside a five-hundred-year-old village six hours south of Marrakech. "The villagers wanted help forming a hospitality project. The whole thing was their idea." In the middle of the desert, Tizkmoudine is not somewhere you stumble across, but as soon as Thierry saw it, he was on board. The rammed-earth buildings were abandoned half a century ago, when the residents moved to a modern village three hundred meters away, and the result is something from another time. The careful restoration of eleven houses ensued, three of which can be slept in. And the surrounding spaces act as a kind of theater that can be set up in all manner of ways. Upon your arrival, there may be a rooftop lunch of caramelized eggplant and couscous and, at dusk, a lantern-lit dinner in a still-abandoned corner of the ancient town. The hot showers run on solar panels, but there are no water pipes or electricity. Everything inside has been created at a grassroots level. Dead trees in the oasis were used to make doors, carpets are woven with palm leaves, and decorations include intricately embroidered palm bark. A trip here is about understanding the story of the community—guests might be invited to a wedding—as well as supporting its regeneration. All the staff are from the village and decide among themselves who does what. Thierry's micro-hospitality is simply the catalyst and has contributed to unlocking economic opportunities such as the village's female weaving cooperative. "Everything we have brought in could be removed in a day. We'd leave no footprint at all." It's a connected and respectful way to travel, looking out for the well-being of future generations. "I spent twenty years serving my guests with the support of communities. And now I want to spend the next twenty years serving communities with the support of my guests."

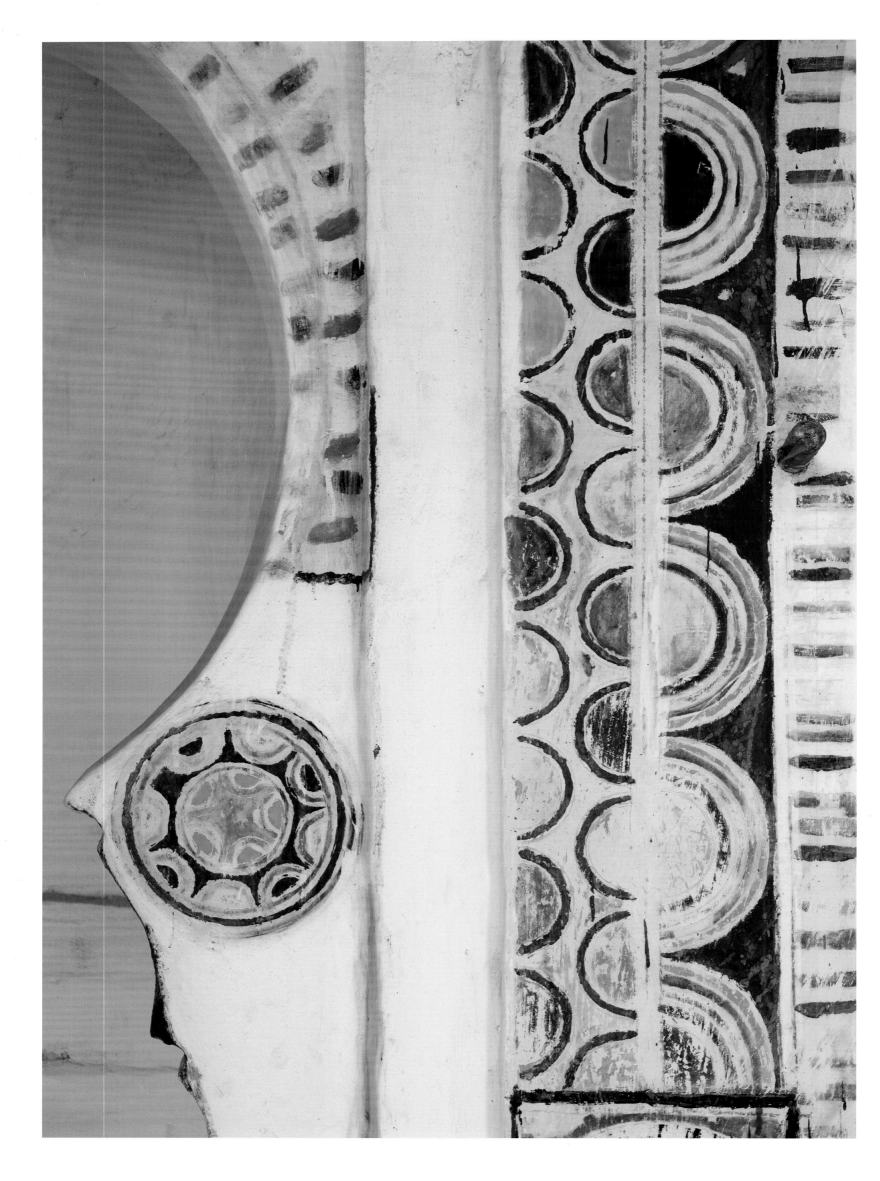

" Everything we have brought in could be removed in a day.
We'd leave no footprint at all. **"**

Villa Cetinale

Owned by the Earl and Countess of Durham

Tuscany, Italy

In its more recent history, Cetinale was something of a Sleeping Beauty, abandoned for many years, overgrown with climbers and weeds, falling ceremoniously into ruin. It was built in 1680 for Pope Alexander VII as a hunting lodge for his nephew Cardinal Flavio Chigi. "The Chigis had so many estates they barely knew what to do with them," says Ned, Earl of Durham, the current owner. "There was a rumor the cardinal had killed someone and felt so guilty he had to escape from Rome." Ned's father, Tony Lambton, himself escaping from disgrace as a young cabinet minister in London—in an episode that involved a couple of prostitutes and a certain amount of weed— felt that, like his hero the writer Somerset Maugham, anyone fleeing from scandal should move abroad immediately. Tony and his mistress Claire Ward first lived in a more modest farmhouse next door. But Tony would look at Cetinale longingly, and one day, hearing it was for sale, bought it. Tony and Claire spent the next thirty years pouring themselves into the house, but almost more attentively to the garden. Tony was wicked, funny, and charismatic, surrounding himself with friends such as Princess Margaret and Mick Jagger as well as a pack of mongrel dogs who would bite guests as and when they felt the desire. "But when he died," says Ned, "there was still a hole in the roof." Marina, Ned's wife, recalls first coming to Cetinale when she was ten. "I remember Tony asking me lots of inappropriate questions, like, if I was a lesbian." By the time Ned inherited it, the house was still both deeply beautiful and deeply shabby—"on the top floor there were just mattresses everywhere." Together with the interior designer Camilla Guinness, who as a neighbor knew Cetinale intimately anyway, they set about a renovation for the family but also to let out the villa exclusively for parties and weddings with the same bohemian bacchanalian streak that has always flowed through its veins. "It was crucial that the work we did on it didn't affect the charm. It would have been quite easy to spoil," says Ned. And the garden continues, demanding and wondrous. There are five gardeners, one who is now eighty, whose own father worked here all his life. "When the wildflowers are out in May, it's stunning," Marina says with a sigh, "but also in autumn, when you can light all the fires." Ned adds, "Cetinale has a certain undefinable magic. I feel like it must be on a ley line. Some houses have it and some don't, this very special energy."

VILLAM CETINALE NVNCVPATAM.
QVÆ. OLIM
ALEXANDRO VII PONTIFICI MAXIMO
VT IMPENSIVS STVDIIS VACARET
IN DELICIIS FVIT
NVNC
FLAVIVS CARDINALIS CHISIVS
ECCLESIA
IN HONOREM DIVI EVSTACHII ERECTA
PLATEIS VNDIQVE CIRCVMDVCTIS
ÆDIBVSQVE INSERVIENTIVM COMMODITATI
CONSTRVCTIS
NNOBILIORLM AMPLIOREMQVE FORMAM REDEGIT
ANNO DOMINI M DC LXXVIII

*66 Cetinale has a certain undefinable magic.
I feel like it must be on a ley line.
Some houses have it and some don't, this very
special energy. 99*

Villa Palladio

Owned by Barbara Miolini

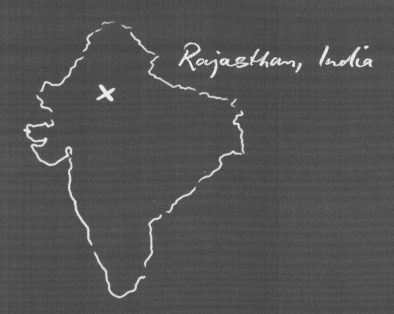

Rajasthan, India

Few are as gung ho with color as the Italian-Swiss Barbara Miolini.
In 2005, she took a sabbatical from her job at a design studio
creating accessories for Diesel, Burberry, and Armani; she'd planned
to head to Africa but detoured to India first on a bit of a whim.
She fell in love, and though the love didn't last forever, she has
never left. "We are still good friends, and my business partner
is his cousin, so it was meant to be." First came the visually
hypnotic Bar Palladio: a peacock-blue restaurant, in the city of
Jaipur, named after Italian Renaissance architect Andrea Palladio,
imagined as a cross between a Venetian café and someplace a maharaja
might hang out. "I'm a little selfish," she says. "I really just
wanted a ready plate of pasta." Barbara asked former fashion and
jewelry designer Marie-Anne Oudejans, who had never worked on
interiors before, to help her with the look: "I just knew she
was the person." Then, determined that people needed a bolt-hole
outside of town but closer to the Pink City than anything already
out there, Barbara went on the hunt to find a pad for a hotel. She
could hardly believe it when she discovered a turreted manor house,
in a forested area with leopards roaming around, only half an
hour's drive into the countryside. Knowing everyone assumed she'd
go big on blue again, and though several friends tried to stop her,
she added a deep cherry red to her palette. "Everything is hand-
painted, which took four months. It's usually the last part of the
project." And the only breather from the brilliant color is on the
breakfast veranda, where the backdrop is white and the first-floor
views of the Aravalli Hills take center stage. Despite the crimson
color scheme, guests claim some of the best nights' sleep of their
lives. "Most people stay here because it's so close to Jaipur, but
when they get here, they struggle to leave. Believe it or not, it's
a break from the noise."

"Most people stay here because it's so close to Jaipur, but when they get here, they struggle to leave. Believe it or not, it's a break from the noise."

The Hall at Bolton Abbey

Owned by the Duke and Duchess of Devonshire

Yorkshire,
England

The Hall at Bolton Abbey breathes quietly among the Yorkshire Moors and, other than the river chuckling at the fingertips of the lawn, if everyone is out walking, fishing, biking, shooting—and you happen to be alone at breakfast, munching toast—even the air molecules feel suspended on a certain type of pause. If everyone is back, then there is a cacophony of sound everywhere. Baths running, a game of sardines getting out of hand, fires roaring, drinks clinking. The first memory Laura Burlington has of the place, before she married William, heir to the Duke of Devonshire, was a Christmas when all of the children were given rollerblades and careened "up and down the passages endlessly at great speed." This was before Laura and decorator Rita Konig had spent two years "trying to modernize it, but without losing any of the idiosyncrasies." She adds, "It was a bit *Bedknobs and Broomsticks.* We are always here for August, but you couldn't have a hot bath without turning the heating on, which was nuts." Now there are putty-bright bathrooms, and tweed carpets in fresh bedrooms, but also still the dark, red-rich opulent glamour of the sitting room, where Debo Devonshire would gossip with the likes of Lucien Freud and Prime Minister Harold Macmillan. The fourteenth-century former gatehouse is available for exclusive use, but it must have been a pressure to get right? "My father-in-law said to me," Laura says with a laugh, "'Whatever we think of it, we'll say it's wonderful, even if it's not!'" Chatsworth and Lismore Castle are also now in the care of the Burlingtons, and for some time there has been an attitude that "it's important to share historic houses. It helps financially but also of course emotionally. There's a new energy for the houses and for the people who work in them." Laura's favorite spot, however, is the walled vegetable garden. "It has a hidden key, and sometimes, in summer, I escape to wander about and eat Victoria plums."

BOLTON ABBEY

LISMORE

Guesses
Make
Misses

Wᵐ Juᵈ of Devonſhire K G Mᵈ Cha ᵗᵉ
Bˢ Clifford dʳ & heˢ of Rᵈ m E of Burlingtᵒ

66 It's important to share historic houses. It helps financially but also of course emotionally. There's a new energy for the houses and for the people who work in them. 99

The Manor House, Babylonstoren

Owned by Karen Roos and Koos Bekker

Simondium,
South Africa

"The rain is always a welcome thing in South Africa," says Karen Roos. "When you hear the rain on the thatch, it's a beautiful sound. But also, the smell of the wet roof is incredible." The reeded thatch atop her H-shaped farmhouse is just one of the traditional methods that has been embraced. Another is the pearly-white lime wash, made out of crushed seashells. "We have to rewash the walls every year, but it's important that we respect the building that way." Karen and husband Koos Bekker have form reviving historic buildings, reimagining Hadspen House in Somerset, England, into the game-changing hotel and country estate the Newt. Here in the Franschhoek Valley, this completely unrestored Cape Dutch manor sits at the heart of Babylonstoren's vineyards. It is part of the action yet still private, tucked away. The house needed considerable attention. They managed to keep the original floors and the yellowwood ceilings. "There were a lot of funny little extensions that we just took off. I wanted to get back to its roots as a very simple homestead," Karen explains. "The main part of the house has three bedrooms—very big drawing rooms, but only three bedrooms. We lived in it for a couple of years, and while I was making it a home, I already had in mind that it could be for other people too." Inside there's little decoration; the look is completely stripped back. "It almost feels like it's still two hundred years ago. There's no real difference except for the bathrooms and kitchen. We inherited some of the beds and the enormous wardrobes that were made for the rooms." The library is where the history comes to life. "There's an eighteenth-century clock that was just left here. And the previous owner gave me a beautiful delft vase that came from the family. I really treasure it. We also have a collection of butterflies entrusted to me by a professor at the university when he turned eighty-five. It is like having a living museum." Lying in bed in the morning, you can see the big swoop of the Swartberg mountain range, sometimes with a dusting of snow on top. And there's often a chicken wobbling on the windowsill—this is a working farm, after all. In addition to the chickens clucking, there are turkeys and sheep. "There was also a donkey that we inherited who did not want to leave. Now we have his fifth-generation foal. Children love him."

66 The rain is always a welcome thing in South Africa. When you hear the rain on the thatch, it's a beautiful sound. But also, the smell of the wet roof is incredible. 99

Mesón Hidalgo

Owned by Laura Kiras

San Miguel de Allende, Mexico

San Miguel de Allende has been on U.S. travelers' radar since the Second World War, when artist Stirling Dickinson invited convalescing GIs to study at the art school for free. "And I had never had any desire to come here for exactly that reason," admits ex—New Yorker Laura Kirar, "but very quickly I discovered that I was so wrong. It's a UNESCO site, insanely beautiful, and packed with incredible craftsmanship." And so the color-mad designer and sculptor, who was based in Mérida and working with artisans across the country, opened a shop in San Miguel to sell their wares. It wasn't until three years later that Laura came across a house off Calle Hidalgo that she couldn't let go. "I know it sounds a little woo-woo when I talk about it, but the truth is that it just had this great energy." The seventeenth-century property has spectacular bones, too-high ceilings, hand-hewn beams, wonderful original wooden doors. And outside, framing the terrace, a wall of straight cacti that, when in bloom, attract a swarm of hummingbirds. A much-revered priest used to live in the house with his sisters, and when he was too old to walk to the parish, the congregation started to queue outside his front window to confess. "People still come by and say they remember him from their childhood." These days, there are three bedrooms to book, each with a bold palette. "I feel really confident using color here. It makes sense. Mexico is my muse." On one wall, a green-and-coral mural has been enlarged from a small painting by Laura. "I am one of these people who thinks I can do everything myself," she says. And it feels like she can: Downstairs is Laura's store, selling woven place mats, copper-plated candelabra, and pottery made in Puebla. But all of the vintage furniture is for sale too. "Guests fall in love with a bedside lamp and then take it home. Luckily, I'm such a hoarder. I could furnish four hotels at this point." Her surreal design eye is apparent in every corner. "I think what makes it different is the sense of humor." It's that and a feeling that it's constantly changing. You might well visit and find she's mixed the whole place up all over again.

" I know it sounds a little woo-woo when I talk about it, but the truth is that it just had this great energy. I feel really confident using color here. It makes sense. Mexico is my muse. "

Biarritz, France

Villa Magnan
Owned by Anne and Jérôme Israël

"Time stopped here in 1936," says Anne Israël of her no-website, Instagram-booking-only château in Biarritz. During the Spanish Civil War, the royal family were said to have taken shelter at Villa Magnan, but it was abandoned when they returned to Madrid. Eighty years later, former stylist and set designer Anne knew immediately that she needed to live here. "It was a Sleeping Beauty in the middle of a big jungle with trees on the roof," and though her husband, cinematographer Jérôme Israël, told her to forget it, three days later they signed the papers and moved out of their Paris home, leaving all of their furniture behind but the kitchen table. Before the move, Anne had viewed the house only completely shuttered and dark. "It's like the villa told me to go slowly because it hadn't seen the sun for so many decades." The colors revealed are the same today, all slightly peeling. Pale pink, pale yellow, pale green, inspired by Cristóbal Balenciaga, one of many bold and brilliant former guests. And while it looks like the furniture inside has been here forever, it took Anne only two weeks to hunt down the interiors at local flea markets. Villa Magnan is something completely fresh for Biarritz. There isn't a whiff of surfer dude on the estate. The family have a donkey, Hector, and a pony, Popo, as well as chickens and peacocks. "I suppose I decided to build my life as a movie," Anne says. Tablescapes at breakfast are different every day, set with elaborate candelabra dripping wax and gourds in various colors, alongside cheeses and croissants and bowls of just-picked plums. Hermès and Chanel have shot inside the villa, and such is the intrigue of the photographs that guests book even before asking what country the property is in. Then, when they arrive, they practically beg to help set the table or do the dishes, and Anne lets them. "I suppose the beauty here is more in the human exchange. I still don't really understand it," she says, musing. "There wasn't a single human in the house for so long. And now the place is just happy to have people to amuse it."

" Time stopped here in 1936. It was a Sleeping Beauty in the middle of a big jungle with trees on the roof. It's like the villa told me to go slowly because it hadn't seen the sun for so many decades. "

Langdon Court

Owned by Donna Ida Thornton
and Robert Walton

Devon, England

"I never know how many bedrooms there are," Donna Ida Thornton admits, having flipped from King's Road denim designer to landlady of the smartest house party in the southwest of England. She'd never even been to Devon before she bought the house. "And we live here now. We have a first-floor corner with our bedroom, dressing room, bathroom, beauty room, and then what we call the tea-and-toast room." The new Australian chatelaine of Langdon Court wasn't planning to take on something so big, but when her restaurateur husband, Robert Walton, came across the particulars, they absolutely fell in love with it. All the furniture had been repossessed by the bank and the rooms stood dusty and neglected, but the bare bones were beautiful. It has a particularly resonant history, too. The Grade II—listed sixteenth-century manor was given to Catherine Parr when King Henry VIII died. In the late 1800s, Richard Cory bought it, and the Prince of Wales and his mistress Lillie Langtry used to come and stay. The Corys, an important Welsh coal-mining family, were big entertainers and very social, throwing lots of shooting parties. "Our neighbor Johnny has all the sales documents, even going back to when it was first built. There's one set of more recent listings pricing it at only £4,000. It's insane." Under Donna's whip-cracking, the house has been done up to the nines, restoring the original ballroom windows, opening spaces, repairing the lath-and-plaster ceilings. The result is vast and sprawling, with a palm court where two lovebirds twitter all day, morning room, drawing room, dining room, film room (with snack room attached), and a library, though of course everyone always ends up crowding into the tiny, glossy yellow chef's nook in the kitchen. But for Donna, it's what's outside that's most important. She's mad for the rose garden: "We had David Austin helping with that. The scent is unbelievable." There's a kitchen garden, huge yews full of crows and rooks, a lavender bank next to the pond where the ducks and geese gather, a heritage orchard heavy with pears. The pathway to the beach is lined with dark ferns and sweet figs, and pheasants roam the grounds. Donna is a convert from her Chelsea days. High fashion has been trumped by horticulture. "Now friends and family will ask, 'What's on your Christmas list?' And I'll say, 'A tree. A tree is all I want right now.'"

" We have a first-floor corner with our bedroom, dressing room, bathroom, beauty room, and then what we call the tea-and-toast room. **"**

Umbria, Italy

Castello di Reschio
Owned by the Bolza family

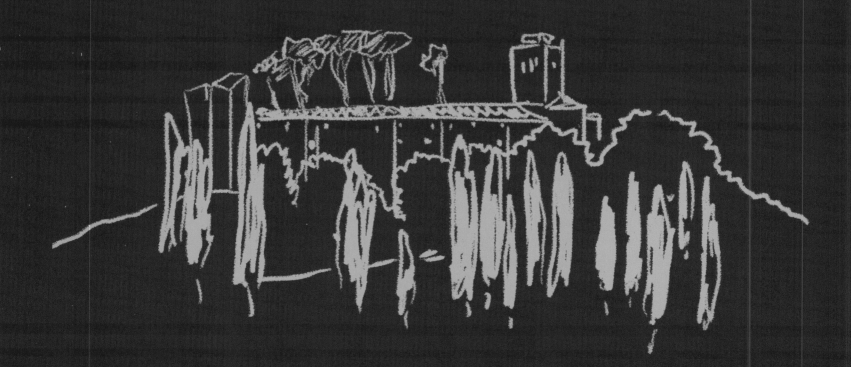

It's a wondrous altered reality at Reschio. The family setup would have been a Bertolucci film in the making: Patriarch Count Antonio Bolza (mad for horses, with a stable of forty Spanish dressage purebreds), architect son Benedikt (spent his teenage holidays measuring the estate's houses and recording their various states of disrepair and ruin), his wildly creative wife, Nencia (grew up in Florence's Palazzo Corsini), and a quintet of children, who, when not studying design or hotel management, return home each summer to write and star in theatrical performances for the guests. The Bolza family entered the scene in 1994 with the purchase of the thousand-year-old castle, fifty or so crumbling sixteenth-century farmhouses, and 3,700 acres of rolling Umbrian farmland, heady with the smell of overgrown wild thyme and broom like an unkempt arcadia. Doing something meaningful—and profitable—with it seemed an impossible task. "You always need a foreigner, don't you?" Benedikt says with a laugh. "My father's Hungarian. My mother's Austrian. We lost all our estates in Hungary after the Second World War, so my father wasn't put off by doing something crazy. It was a way to regrow our roots." Benedikt and Nencia, who for years wandered about with a pet canary in her hair, brought their children up in the wreck of the castle. "It was far too big for us. We had a lot of guest bedrooms. They didn't have any heating, but they looked okay in summer. In the winter they were not so nice. When it rained, the water came through the roof." It's a far cry from the way Reschio is now. The castle, after three and a half years of toil and graft, is extravagantly reimagined as a hotel and, with such lively, soulful custodians, has become a thoroughbred that ambitiously and vivaciously dances to its own exemplary tune. Twenty-nine of the abandoned farm buildings, most with no roofs, have been revived to megawatt villas, owned by international designers and tech pioneers, sold at a rate of around one a year, and some rented out when the owners are not in residence. It's a turbocharged project of serious intentions and integrity, as well as deeply considered design. And what, then, does the future hold for Reschio? "Protection, protection, protection" is Benedikt's mantra. "And then of course there's so much more to restore. I've only done half the houses. It will go on for a long time."

66 It was far too big for us. We had a lot of guest bedrooms. They didn't have any heating, but they looked okay in summer. In the winter, they were not so nice. When it rained, the water came through the roof. 99

Achillea Filipendula

Achillea

Rosmarin

Elicrisio

Properties

Aristide Hotel

27 Babagiotou Street, 84100 Hermoupolis,
Syros, Greece
+ 30 698 662 4881
hotelaristide.com
welcome@hotelaristide.com

Bethlen Estates

157 Cris, Judetul Mures, Danes-Criş 547201,
Transylvania, Romania
+ 40 767 374 998
bethlenestates.com
booking@bethlenestates.com

Boath House

Auldearn, Nairn IV12 5TE, United Kingdom
+ 44 (0) 1667 454 896
boath-house.com
info@boath-house.com

Braganza House

Ussaiddamalwatta, Mihiripenna Road, Talpe,
Sri Lanka
braganza-house.com
chloe@eandainteriors.com

Casa na Terra

7200-718 Reguengos de Monsaraz, Portugal
+ 351 964 362 816
silentliving.pt/houses/casa-na-terra
booking@silentliving.pt

Castello di Reschio

Tabaccaia di Reschio, 06060 Lisciano
Niccone, Perugia, Italy
+ 39 075 844 362
reschio.com
reservations@reschio.com

Castle Elvira

Via Andrano, 73019 Trepuzzi, Lecce, Puglia, Italy
+ 39 0832 177 82 59
castleelvira.com
info@castleelvira.com

Cristine Bedfor

Carrer de la Infanta, 19, 07702 Mahón,
Menorca, Spain
+ 34 971 635 502
cristinebedforhotel.com
mahon@cristinebedfor.com

Langdon Court

Adam's Lane, Down Thomas, Plymouth, Devon
PL9 0DY, United Kingdom
+ 44 (0) 7484 909 150
langdoncourtmanor.com
hello@langdoncourtmanor.com

Le Mas de Chabran

Chemin du Mas de Chabran,
13520 Maussane-les-Alpilles, France
+ 33 (0) 6 51 52 09 99
masdechabran.com
reservations@masdechabran.fr

Lopud 1483

Lopud, Dubrovnik, Croatia
lopud1483.com
booking@lopud1483.com

Maana Homes

427-18 Myohoin Maekawacho, Maana Kiyomizu,
Higashiyama Ward, Kyoto 605-0932, Japan
48103 Nishitachibanacho, Maana Kamo,
Higashiyama Ward, Kyoto 605-0907, Japan
33-6 Chudoji Kitamachi, Maana Kyoto, Shimogyo
Ward, Kyoto 600-8812, Japan
maanahomes.com
stay@maanahomes.com

Mesón Hidalgo

Hidalgo 19, Zona Centro, 37700 San Miguel
de Allende, Guanajuato, Mexico
+ 52 415 196 0536
mesonhidalgo.com
digame@mesonhidalgo.com

Passalacqua

Via Besana, 59, 22010 Moltrasio, Como, Italy
+ 39 031 44311
passalacqua.it
reservations@passalacqua.it

Taylor River Lodge

10931 County Road 742, Almont, CO 81210, USA
+ 1 888 308 4332
elevenexperience.com/taylor-river-lodge
reservations@elevenexperience.com

The Hall at Bolton Abbey

Bolton Abbey Estate, Skipton, North
Yorkshire BD23 6AL, United Kingdom
+ 44 1756 718112
thehallandlismorecastle.com
info@thehallatboltonabbey.co.uk

The Manor House, Babylonstoren

Klapmuts Simondium Road, Simondium, 7670,
South Africa
+ 27 (0) 21 863 3852
babylonstoren.com
enquiries@babylonstoren.com

Tizkmoudine

Tizkmoudine, Morocco
700000heures.com/tizkmoudine
contact@700000heures.com

Villa Cetinale

Strada di Cetinale, 9, 53018 Sovicille,
Siena, Italy
+ 39 0577 311147
villacetinale.com
booking@villacetinale.com

Villa Mabrouka

1 Sidi Bouknadel, Tangier, Morocco, 90000
+ 212 (0) 808 52 6436
villamabrouka.com
contact@villamabrouka.com

Villa Magnan

11 Rue de Mouriscot, 64200 Biarritz
+ 33 9 51 26 66 81
instagram.com/villamagnan

Villa Palladio

Abhay Niwas Palace, Jamdoli Chouraha,
Jaipur, Rajasthan 302031, India
+ 91 141 2969762
villa-paladio-jaipur.com
info@villa-paladio-jaipur.com

Acknowledgments

The publisher would like to specially thank: Tabitha Joyce, Melinda Stevens, and Issy von Simson.

The publisher would like to thank the following: Aristide Hotel: Giorgos Alifragis, Oana Aristide, the Aristide family, Justin Tyler Close, Laurent Fabre, George Negrea, Alexandros Petrakis, and Francesca Saffari; Bethlen Estates: Countess Gladys Bethlen, Count Nikolaus Bethlen, and the Bethlen family; BIRD Travel Public Relations: Milly Barr and Daisy Bird; Boath House: Liam Black, Beth Evans, Jonny Gent, and Russell Potter; Braganza House: Mo Arpi and Chlöe Elkerton; Casa na Terra: Rui Cardoso, Nelson Garrido, Amanda Ho, Silje Kvernerland, Manuel Aires Mateus, Alexandra Ramos, and João Rodrigues; Castello di Reschio: Count Benedikt Bolza and the Bolza family; Castle Elvira: Giacomo Attanasio, Harvey B-Brown, Mark Cocksedge, Rei Moon, and Steven Riseley; Enrico Costantini; Cristine Bedfor: Cristina Lozano, Daniel Schaefer, and Cristina Soto; Fraser Communications: Melis Kurum, Dani Loewensohn, and Méabh Page; Langdon Court: Donna Ida Thornton, Robert Walton, and Nico Wills; Le Mas de Chabran: Alexis Armanet, Alain Meylan, and Liliana Meylan; Lopud 1483: Francesca Thyssen-Bornemisza and Igor Zacharov; Maana Homes: Jonas Bjerre-Poulsen, Irene Chang, Dennis-Kyōsuke Ginsig, Renee Kemps, Cieran Murphy, Yohei Sasakura, Amy Tang, Hana Tsukamoto, Mitsuru Wakabayashi, and Sonny Zehnder; Mesón Hidalgo: Irene Amaya, Laura Kirar, and Pepe Molina; Passalacqua: Stefano Butturini, Valentina De Santis, the De Santis family, Stefan Giftthaler, Mariela Medina, Ricky Monti, and Ruben Ortiz; Perowne International: Hannah Boucher, Adam Budhram, Emma Fowler, Julia Perowne, and Aiden Ronson; Taylor River Lodge: Blake and Chad Pike; The Hall at Bolton Abbey: Anna Batchelor, Laura Burlington, the Duke and Duchess of Devonshire; The Manor House, Babylonstoren: Koos Bekker, Greg Cox, and Karen Roos; Tizkmoudine: Shin Jinushi, Stéphanie Moulin, Thierry Teyssier, and the villagers of Tizkmoudine; Philip Vile; Villa Cetinale: the Countess of Durham, the Earl of Durham, Karen Howes, Simon Upton, and Manuel Zublena; Villa Mabrouka: Jasper Conran, Jessica Harris, and Andrew Montgomery; Villa Magnan: Anne, Jérôme, Melvin, and Zélie Israël; Villa Palladio: Barbara Miolini and Atul Pratap Chauhan.

Additional thanks to: Aristide Hotel: Jasmin Aristide, Simona Aristide, and Anouk Aumont; Bethlen Estates: Countess Theodora Bethlen and local shepherds Florin and Ion; Castello di Reschio: Countess Donna Nencia Bolza; Le Mas de Chabran: Jerry Goede; Lopud 1483: Marino Radić; Passalacqua: Beppe Cetti and Alessandro Rinaldi; The Hall at Bolton Abbey: Alice B-B, Peter Smith, and Mark Whitehead; Tizkmoudine: Afaf Ait Said, Fadma Hmairrou, and Khadija Oumanssour.

Credits

Pages: 10-11, 12, 13, 14, 15 (top left, top right, bottom left), 17, 18, 19, 20, 21, 22-23: © Lopud 1483; p. 15 (bottom right): © Igor Zacharov; pp. 26-27, 28 (top left, top right, bottom left, bottom right), 32-33 © Nelson Garrido; p. 29: © Amanda Ho; p. 30: © Silje Kvernerland; p. 34: © Rui Cardoso; pp. 35, 44, 46: © Enrico Costantini; pp. 38, 41: © Mariela Medina; pp. 39, 43, 47, 49, 50: © Ruben Ortiz; p. 40: © Ricky Monti; p. 42: © Stefan Giftthaler; p. 51: © Stefano Butturini; pp. 54-55, 56, 57, 58, 59 (top left, top right, bottom left, bottom right), 60, 62 (top left, top right, bottom left, bottom right), 63, 288, 289, 291, 294-295, 296-297, 298: © Philip Vile; pp. 66, 71 (bottom right): © Giorgos Alifragis; pp. 67, 71 (top left): © Alexandros Petrakis; pp. 68-69: © Justin Tyler Close; p. 71 (top right): © Laurent Fabre; pp. 71 (bottom left), 73: © George Negrea; p. 72: © Francesca Saffari; pp. 76, 77, 78-79, 81, 82, 83, 84-85, 86, 87, 88, 89: © Villa Mabrouka/Photographer: Andrew Montgomery; pp. 92-93, 104: © Liam Black; pp. 94-95, 96, 97, 99, 100, 101, 102-103, 106, 107: © Beth Evans; p. 98: © Boath House; pp. 110, 111, 112, 113, 114, 115, 116: © Daniel Schaefer; pp. 120-121, 122, 123, 126, 127 (top left, top right, bottom left, bottom right): © Alexis Armanet; p. 125: © Mark Elst; pp. 130, 132 (top right), 134, 135: © Mark Cocksedge; pp. 131, 132 (top left, bottom left, bottom right), 133, 136, 138, 139: © Rei Moon; pp. 143, 144, 145, 146-147, 148, 149 (top left, top right, bottom left, bottom right), 150, 151, 152, 153, 154-155: © Braganza House/Photographer: Mo Arpi; pp. 158-159, 160, 161, 162, 163, 164, 165, 166, 168-169: © Eleven Taylor River Lodge; pp. 172-173: © Sonny Zehnder and Dennis-Kyōsuke Ginsig; pp. 174, 181 (bottom left): © Cieran Murphy; p. 175: © Yohei Sasakura; pp. 176-177: © Mitsuru Wakabayashi; p. 178: © Renee Kemps; p. 180: © Maana Homes; p. 181 (top left, top right): © Amy Tang; (bottom right): © Jonas Bjerre-Poulsen; pp. 184-185, 186, 187, 188, 189 (top left, top right, bottom left, bottom right), 190-191, 192, 194-195: © 700,000 Heures; pp. 198, 199, 200, 201, 202-203, 205 (top left, top right, bottom left, bottom right), 208: © Manuel Zublena; pp. 204, 207, 209: © Simon Upton; pp. 212, 213, 215, 216, 217, 218, 219: © Atul Pratap Chauhan; pp. 222 (top left, top right, bottom left, bottom right), 223, 224, 225, 226-227, 228, 229 (top left, top right, bottom left, bottom right), 230, 231, 232: © Anna Batchelor; pp. 236-237: © Babylonstoren; pp. 238, 239, 240, 241, 242 (top left, top right, bottom left, bottom right) 244, 245: © Greg Cox / Bureaux; pp. 248-249, 251 (top left, top right, bottom left, bottom right), 252-253, 254, 255, 256-257: © Pepe Molina; pp. 260-261, 262, 263, 264, 266 (top left, top right, bottom left, bottom right), 267, 268, 269, 273: © Melvin Israël; pp. © 270-271, 272: © Villa Magnan; pp. 276-277, 278, 279, 281, 282 (top left, top right, bottom left, bottom right), 283, 284-285: © Nico Wills; pp. 292, 293 (top left, top right, bottom left, bottom right), 299: © Reschio.

Every possible effort has been made to identify and contact all rights holders and obtain their permission for work appearing in these pages. Any errors or omissions brought to the publisher's attention will be corrected in future editions.

Front cover design and endpages:
© Assouline.
*Back cover tip-on (clockwise from top
left):* © Philip Vile; © Alexis Armanet;
© Manuel Zublena; © Sonny Zehnder and
Dennis-Kyōsuke Ginsig

© 2024 Assouline Publishing
3 Park Avenue, 27th floor
New York, NY 10016 USA
Tel: 212-989-6769 Fax: 212-647-005
assouline.com

Editor: Léana Esch
Creative director: Jihyun Kim
Designer and illustrator: Dylan Brackett
Senior photo editor: Andrea Ramírez Reyes
Junior photo researcher: Teddy Bensimon

Printed in Italy at Grafiche Milani.
ISBN: 9781649803313

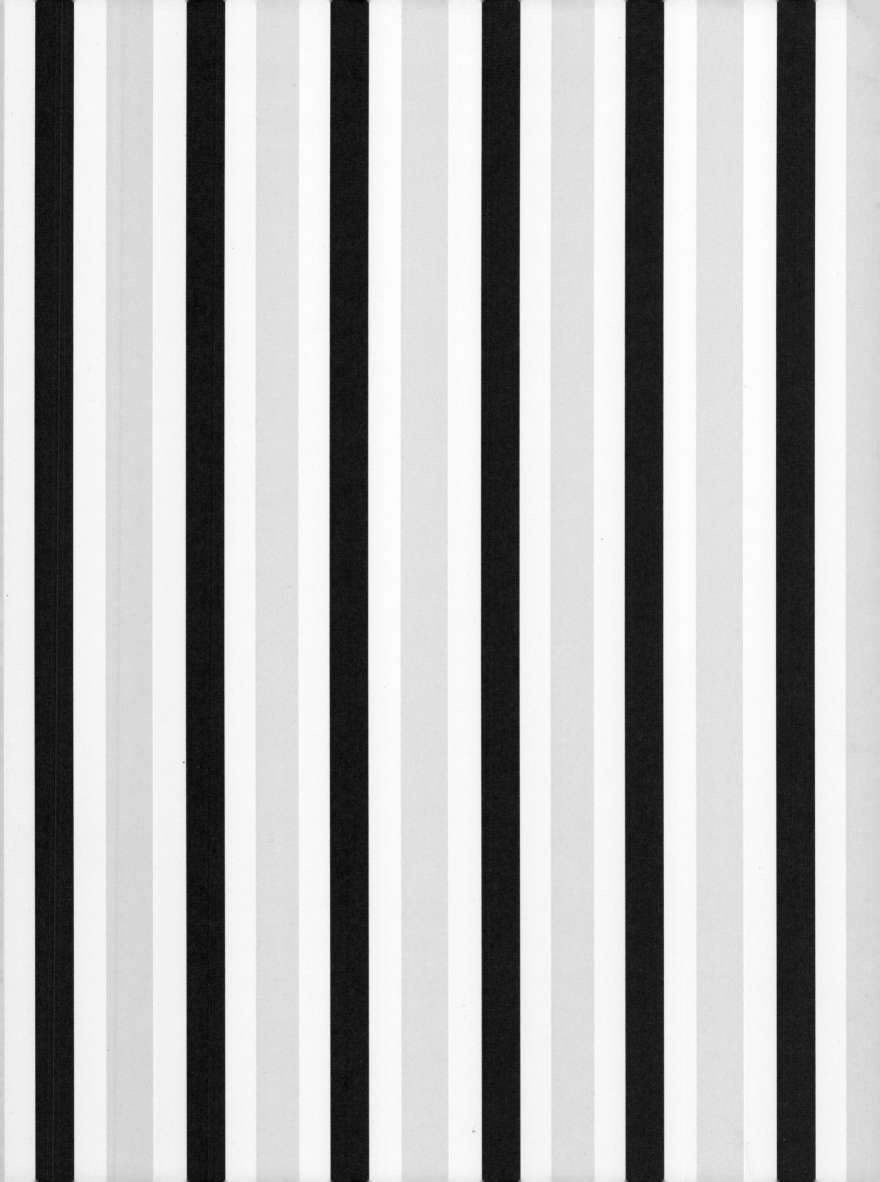

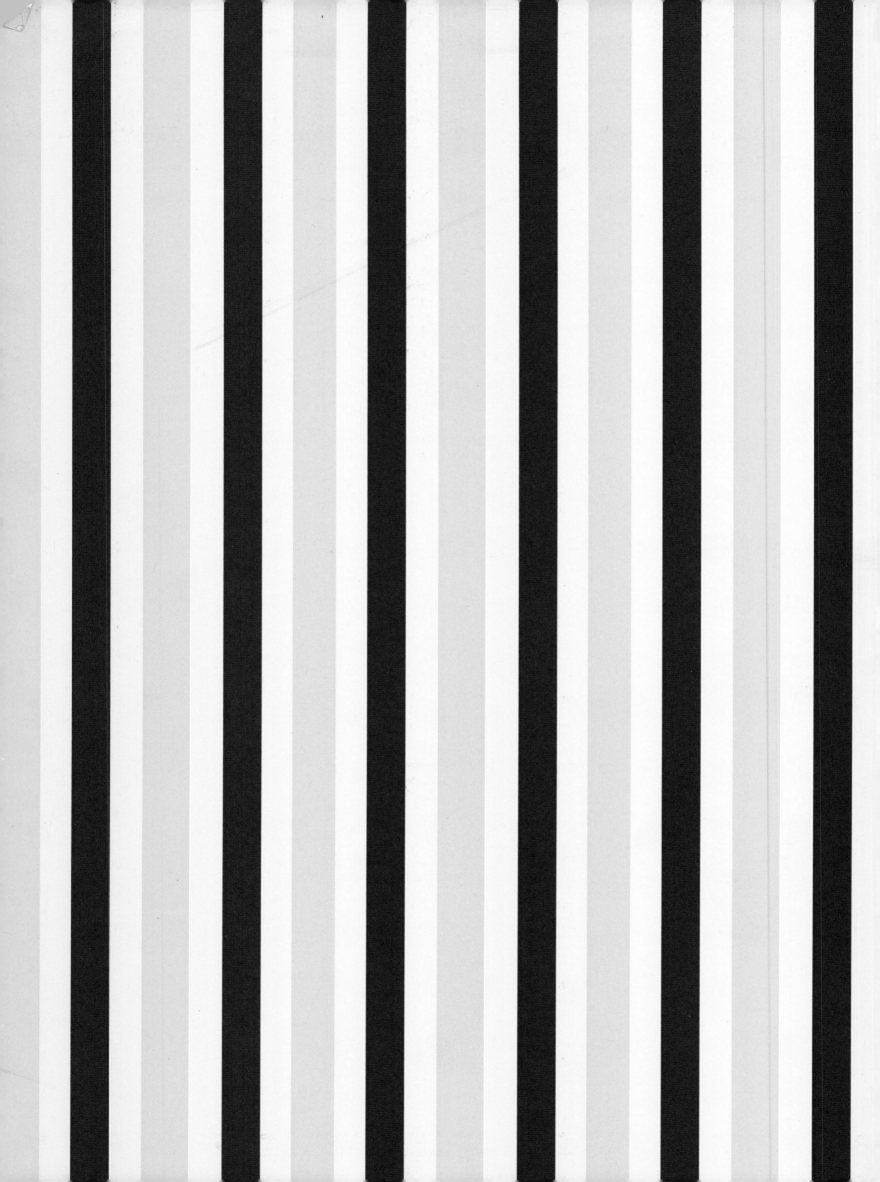